My not so
Poetic Life

My not so
Poetic Life

DEVEN DONOVAN

TATE PUBLISHING
AND ENTERPRISES, LLC

Published by Tate Publishing & Enterprises, LLC
127 E. Trade Center Terrace | Mustang, Oklahoma 73064 USA
1.888.361.9473 | www.tatepublishing.com

Tate Publishing is committed to excellence in the publishing industry. The company reflects the philosophy established by the founders, based on Psalm 68:11,
"The Lord gave the word and great was the company of those who published it."

Book design copyright © 2016 by Tate Publishing, LLC. All rights reserved.
Cover design by Joshua Rafols
Interior design by Richell Balansag

Published in the United States of America

ISBN: 978-1-68270-145-4
1. Poetry / Subjects & Themes / General
2. Poetry / Subjects & Themes / Family
15.11.04

I'd like to thank all my friends and family for we've been through a lot good and bad,but I love you all and am thankful we've stuck together through out it all. But most of all my son Tyler who is my greatest accomplishment,e ncouragement,and inspiration. He's the reason I've learnt what it means to love unconditionally.

Ten little fingers, ten little toes
Oh, look at that cute little nose!
Looking up at me blowing little baby bubbles,
oh, boy my heart was in trouble 'cause
that's when I knew
I'd never love anyone like I love you
Holding tightly your little blanket
'cause you didn't want anyone to take it
Seems like yesterday you were just ten
with your daddy's little grin
Guess I can't stop you from getting
older 'cause everyone grows
It's just the way it goes
I just hope you remember to respect your elders;
don't forget your manners
And to all women, show the same courtesy
you'd want for me
It's amazing seeing the great man you're becoming
I hope one day I'll be able to see
your own little version of
ten little fingers
ten little toes
and your child's cute little nose

I remember, even if you didn't think I
would, the screaming and crying.
Hiding under the bed with my
puppy and my baby brother.
Holding on to each other, scared and crying.
I remember, even if you didn't think I would,
the late-night hospital trips; lying,
because you claimed to have tripped,
leaving you black and blue
knowing that wasn't true.
I remember, even if you didn't think I would,
wondering why we had to live this way,
why we had to stay.
Why you couldn't believe we could just leave.
These are the things I remember even
if you didn't think I would.

Deven Donovan

Baby, pack
A bag
'Cause I'm constantly
Fighting for an imaginary
Love
Is it not enough?
I've given all I got
Your once-warm touch
That I miss so much
Has turned cold
And you no longer hold
Me tight
At night
So, baby, pack
A bag
If you need
You can tell yourself it isn't you
It's me
If that's what you want to
Believe

You and I may never be, but for tonight we are complete.
So for now, let's just try to look in each
other's eyes without any disguise.
And dance like it's our only chance to be.
Tonight, let's stand heart-to-heart, hoping
that we may never have to part.
Tonight, I say to you that for me it'll just be you,
because your love
Is enough.

Deven Donovan

Do you hear the heavens crying?
Do you hear God sighing?
Because this wasn't his plan in the beginning
I wonder if he's ever doubted our creation
It's no revelation
How there's no love
For each other
Or respect for one another
But it won't be this way forever
There's no need to fear
Because his will hear
Your prayers
And even when we feel
We cannot take any more
We can be sure
In his own time
Everything will be fine

Don't tell me what to wear
Or how to do my hair
I just don't care
I used to think
Without you I'd sink
It might've taken me a little longer
But I've grown stronger
And I know I will be just fine
Without you in my life
Yes, I'll be okay on my own
Because I have grown
And I'm ready
To be free
Of you controlling me

Deven Donovan

Every tear I've shed
Every hurtful thing you've said
Plays on in my mind
You say you're sorry
That you don't deserve me
Just like all the other times
You've lied
My eyes are sore
My heart can't take much more
So hear my voice
Make a choice
To change
Your ways
Or leave
So I can be free

Fishing with Grandpa
With his handmade sugarcane poles and line
I really miss those times
Then helping Grandma cook it in her own special way
I really miss those days
Reminiscing with them
Of way back when
They were younger
Life was more simple
People were more humble
They've been gone for years now
But I can't forget how
To me they would sing
Telling me I could be anything
So loving and kind
I really wouldn't mind
Having one more day
Fishing with Grandpa
And cooking with Grandma

Deven Donovan

For those depressed, suppressed
Souls with hearts full of holes
I've been there
Where it feels like no one would care
If you were here
Or would just disappear
To not understand why
You just want to cry
Why my happiness doesn't last?
Why I feel like I'm falling fast?
Why don't they understand?
The demands
Within me
Or see
And look away
From the struggles I have every day
To those who feel this way
And don't know what to do
I empathize with you
You're not alone
I've been there too

Good-byes are hard, but I'm going to try to let you go
because I know,
good-byes are not forever.
But I'll never forget you
and everything you used to do.
I can still see your smile
even though it's been a while
I can still hear your voice calling my name
saying the same
little things you used to
even though you left too soon
I'll see you again
and then it will be
as if you never left me
because good-byes are never forever

Deven Donovan

Have we lost our fire?
That strong desire
For each other
Would you even care
If we weren't a pair?
Tell me what's it going to take
To make
This last
Like we were in the past
Do you even want to try
One more time?
After all we've been through
Am I still enough for you?
Or is it too late
To make
You and me
Be
What we
Once were

I need you to know you came to me by surprise,
but I finally knew real love when I looked into your eyes.
When everything seems to be going
wrong, it's never too long
before I see it will all be fine.
Because your love is all mine, and no matter what I do,
I know your love will always be true.
And I will always have you.
So I need you to know,
I will always be by your side,
and when you feel all alone
just know you can always come home and feel secure
because my love for you is pure.
So please never forget as you grow
old, these are the things I need you to know.

Deven Donovan

I remember the day
I got the news
about you
I was nervous
and scared
Unprepared
for the changes
I was about to make
But I was also
excited
Overjoyed
the day they said
"It's a boy!"
All my concerns
and worries went
away
that warm
summer day
in July
when they put you by my side

I should've listened
Should've questioned
Your intentions
Then I wouldn't be
In this situation
I need respect
Not neglect
I want my words
To be heard
And not ignored
Is that too much
To ask?
Can you at least act
As if
You care
Are you even aware
Of my feelings
I've been concealing

Deven Donovan

I was just eighteen
I was rushing to get ready 'cause I didn't want to be late
For our first date
You were the guy of my dreams.
And it seems
Like just yesterday you were asking my dad for my hand,
'Cause you wanted to be my man.
We've had our highs and lows
But we have always chosen
To get around
Our ups and downs
Eighteen years later
There's no greater love
To rise above

I was only seven
But I was given
One more chance
At life
Because I survived
The doctor said I may never walk
Or talk
Again
That's when
I knew it wouldn't be
Easy
For me
I was just a little girl
In what felt like a cruel world
I heard the whispers
I saw the stares
Did they not think I'd care?
Did they not think I'd see?
The way they looked at me
Maybe if they knew
What I had been through
It would've been different
People would've been more compassionate
I was only seven
But I was given
One more chance to live

Deven Donovan

I will not be contained
I have no restraints
Tell me no
And I'll show
You
A thing
Or two
Don't confuse
My kindness
For weakness
I will stand
Firm
Don't make demands
Of me
Or promises
You can't keep
Because over you
I will no longer weep

I'm getting a little stronger
Day by day
It's taken me a little longer
Than it should
But if I could
I'd erase
Your face
From my memory
And let these feelings be a part of history
But you're a part of my past
That wasn't meant to last
But at least from what I now know
It'll help me to grow
To be stronger

Deven Donovan

I'm not going to waste
Another day
Another tear
On the fear
This won't work
'Cause I'm worth
More
Than you're
Giving
It's time I start living
For me
Even if that means
You leave

It was all happening so fast
With a tight grasp
On the steering wheel
Praying this wasn't real
Continuously pressing the brakes
Please don't let us die
Because of someone else's mistake
Watching both our lives
Flash before my eyes
Thinking what was I going to do
If I lost you
Seemed like forever before I gained control
As we were pushed off the road
Don't know if I ever told you
I thank God everyday
We were able to walk away
That day

Deven Donovan

It's time I start living for me
Time to be
Happy
One day
You will see
All I can do
You can be certain
I am determined
To show
My goals
Are more than dreams
To me
Because I'm ready
To be happy

My dreams
May not seem
Like much to
You
But I will make them come true
Because I believe
I will
Succeed
In what I do

My face was so red
From what she said
My face was blushing
My heart racing. You overheard my secret
Guess she couldn't keep it
That I was into you
Were you expecting it?
Do you feel the same?
Or is this just a game?
So what do you think?
Should we try this thing?
Or leave it as it is
And just stay friends

Deven Donovan

My feet ache
My legs shake
I don't know how much more I can take
This pain is unreal
If only, for once, I could feel
Okay
Even if it's only for a day
If I could sleep through the night
Without every muscle getting tight
Trying hard to win this fight
I'd be ever so thankful
Ever so grateful
Just for one day
Without this pain

My summer crush
Just
Lasted until spring
But the memories
Bring
Back feelings
Of
Having my first love
The butterflies
Being so shy
The first time
Your hand touched mine
The phone calls that lasted all night long
Just talking until dawn
The memories I have
Of
My first love
My summer crush

Deven Donovan

My weatherman quit raining on my heart
Don't you know how much it hurts?
You're like a tornado
Everywhere you go
Destroying whatever is in your path
Never looking back
My weatherman
You're like a hurricane
With your games
Blowing through my life
Playing with my mind
My weatherman, you're like a tsunami
Leaving me
In an ocean of tears
My weatherman, you're like an earthquake
Tearing me down
Not admitting your mistakes
My weatherman, I can no longer
Ride out what has formed
From your storms

Once upon a time, there was one boy and one girl,
and nothing else mattered in their world
They said I was too young
And we were wrong
to think we'd last very long
But they couldn't see we were strong
Once upon a time, there was one boy and one girl,
and nothing else mattered in their world
And if they could only see
we were meant to be
there'd be no doubting me
Now four years have gone by
and we
are now three
And it all began with
Once upon a time, there was one boy and one girl,
and nothing else mattered in their world.

Deven Donovan

Sitting in the waiting room
Of the doctor's office
Hoping you don't notice
'Cause I'm trying hard to hide
The tears in my eyes
Praying for good news
There's so much to lose
The doctor comes in with the answer
It's cancer
Not what we wanted to hear
Our greatest fear
We all try to stay hidden
No one can escape
Or know their fate
All we can do is pray
And live day for day

Sorry, not sorry
You say
Why you got to be that way?
You need to change your attitude
Start showing some gratitude
Sorry, not sorry
You say
Why you got to be that way?
After all I do
For you
How can you be so rude?
Sorry, not sorry
You say
Why you got to be that way?
Taking me for granted
Not the life I wanted
So to you
Sorry, not sorry
I say
I will not live this way

Deven Donovan

Thoughts of you run through my mind
Every now and then
Time and time again
Every time
I hear that song
You sang to me on the phone
A long time ago
Thoughts of you run through my mind
Every now and then
Time and time again
I still remember
Your silly humor
Like when we went to see
A movie
And your hand
Just happened to land
On mine
Thoughts of you run through my mind
Every now and then
Time and time again
But I couldn't stay
We moved away
And I'm left with
Thoughts of you

What am I supposed to do
When there's no pleasing you?
When you think your wife
Can never be right
When you say I'm too fat
Then I'm too thin
Now I'm too fat again
What do you want from me?
Who am I supposed to be?
Why can't you just accept me
And be supportive
Let me live
Build me up
When I'm down
And not be the thorn in my crown
Just help me
To be happy

Deven Donovan

What do you do
When the one who's hurt you
Suddenly needs you?
What do you do
When your memories of them
Are unhappy thoughts
Feelings you've fought
To forget
Not have to relive it
But now they're alone and sick
What do you do?
I'm so confused
It's not easy to
Always do
What is right
When it's not all black or white
What do you do
When the one who's hurt you
Suddenly needs you

When will the cycle end
Instead of begin again?
After all we've been through
How can you
Continue
This way
Every day
And not feel shame
When you hurt her?
Because you know it's not what she deserves
So I beg of you to end this abuse
When there is no use
Of
Letting the cycle begin again
When you can make it end

Deven Donovan

Why did you stay?
Why didn't you take us away?
You weren't they only one black and blue
We had bruises too
Always walking on eggshells
Was our hell
Trying not to
Say or do
The wrong thing
Never looking
Forward to the weekend
'Cause that meant he'd
Be drinking again
Never knowing what to expect
Always living in fear
Was a secret we all kept

Why does it seem
People are all so mean
Everyone is worried about
Everyone else
Instead of themselves
Always trying to tear each other down
Are they proud
Of their actions?
Does it give them some sort of satisfaction?
Or are they just so unhappy
And are lacking
The love and support
They need
To succeed?

Deven Donovan

Why must we live this way?
why do you say the things you say?
why do I let you tear me down?
why can't you see how your words affect me?
why can't we just leave
and not grieve something we once had
that is ending so bad
why try to change someone from what they have become?
why keep asking why when it's time to just move on

You are
My alpha
My omega
My beginning
My end
My lifelong friend
Since I first held you in my arms
When you grasped my finger
You gained control of my heart
You are
Why I am living
My reason for breathing
Before you
I never understood
How I could
Love someone
Unconditionally
Unselfishly
You are
My alpha
My omega
My beginning
My end
My lifelong friend

Deven Donovan

You say
It's your way
Or the highway
And by now I should know
If not, I could go
But that door
Was made for more
Than just me
And you could also leave
So if you choose
Not to lose
Me
You need
To see
What's gone wrong
And fight
To make this right

You want her
Under the condition
That she
Do and listen
To everything you say
But what if one day
Your words won't matter
And you won't be able to
Flatter her
Like you did before
It won't matter
Anymore
You want her
If you can control
And have a tight hold
Of her life
But it won't last too much longer
'Cause she's getting stronger

Deven Donovan

You've made a promise to me
Before God and all our family
And friends
To love and care for me
To the end
But when you don't get your way
The things you say
Go from love to hate
I keep telling myself everything
Will be okay
I just have to be patient
And wait
You'll change
But I get blamed
For the things you say
I make you act that way
I never thought
I'd get caught
Up in
This life we've been living

BABY DON'T FALL

My little man
Is learning to walk
And to stand alone
I say to him be careful
Baby don't fall

He's a little older now
Learning how
To ride a bike on his own
I say to him be careful
Baby don't fall

Now a teenager
I've taught him to be
On his best behavior
And on the wrong path
I say to him be careful
Baby don't fall

And if one day he meets
Someone who doesn't appreciate
How great
Of a person he is
I'll say to him be careful
Baby don't fall.

Deven Donovan

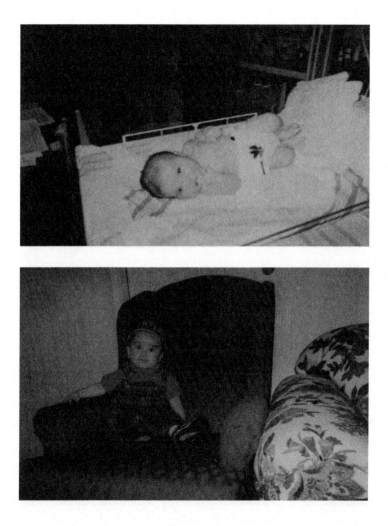

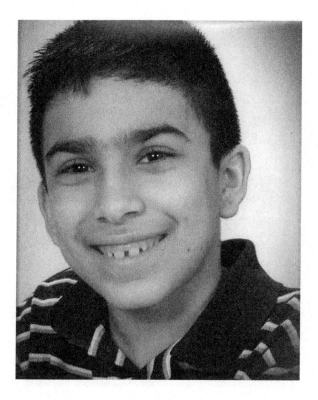